Releasing
Hope

To: Jen,

May the God of hope fill you with
all joy and peace as you trust in Him,
so that you may overflow with hope
by the power of the Holy Spirit.

— Romans 15:13

J. V. Wallace
7-19-2014

Releasing
Hope

through a collection of paintings with
words of encouragement & verses of Scripture

Jennifer V. Wallace

TATE PUBLISHING
AND ENTERPRISES, LLC

Published by Tate Publishing & Enterprises, LLC
127 E. Trade Center Terrace | Mustang, Oklahoma 73064 USA
1.888.361.9473 | www.tatepublishing.com

Tate Publishing is committed to excellence in the publishing industry. The company reflects the philosophy established by the founders, based on Psalm 68:11,
"The Lord gave the word and great was the company of those who published it."

Published in the United States of America

ISBN: 978-1-62994-302-2
1. Religion/Christian Life/Inspirational
2. Religion/Christian Life/Devotional
13.10.03

Dedication

This book is dedicated to my children: Shawn, Seth, Virginia, David and to the Body of Christ at Restoration Outreach Church. Thank you for all of your encouragement, help, and prayers. I am amazed at how truly blessed I am to have you walking with me during this season of my life.

This book is also dedicated to all of those God will encounter and transform through the following pages. May He release hope that brings peace, healing, and freedom!

Introduction

Hope is a way of thinking, a confident expectation. It is a view of life that is birthed out of believing in the goodness of God and His promises. God designed hope to give life to your body, mind, and soul while you wait and trust in Him. It is part of how His kingdom operates, is an extension of faith, and comes from being filled with His joy and peace. This hope gives you courage and strength as you walk each day with God.

Releasing Hope is a collection of thirty paintings with words of encouragement and verses of Scripture. Each one was created from fellowshiping and partnering with God in order to reveal His heart. So as you enjoy this devotional book, let God speak to you, bless you, and stir up hope deep within you!

Walking the path of life with God is a process
Daily seek Him - Abide in His Word
Trust Him - Step out in faith
Experiencing God surrounds you
producing an intimate relationship with Him

But I am like a green olive tree in the house of God;
I trust in the mercy of God forever and ever.
I will praise you forever, because You have done it;
in the presence of Your saints
I will wait on Your name, for it is good.

Psalm 52:8-9

Abiding Faith

Jesus came to give you abundant life
His extravagant love heals your soul
Creating health & prosperity in all things
Growing in you His love, peace,
joy & hope to overflowing

The thief does not come except to steal,
and to kill, and to destroy.
I have come that they may have life,
and that they may have it more abundantly.

John 10:10

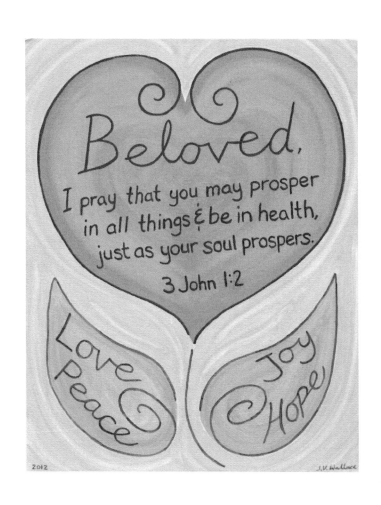

Beloved,

I pray that you may prosper in all things & be in health, just as your soul prospers.

3 John 1:2

Love Peace

Joy Hope

2012

J.V. Wallace

Abundant Life

God is growing you
Shaking what can be shaken
Lay aside those things that hinder
your relationship with Him
Endure this process of
God's purifying fire by faith

Therefore, since we are receiving a kingdom
which cannot be shaken,
let us have grace,
by which we may serve God acceptably
with reverence and godly fear.
For our God is a consuming fire.

Hebrews 13:28-29

Cannot Be Shaken

In the Lord's presence & through Holy Spirit
God creates, renews, restores, & upholds
Growing in you a clean heart,
a steadfast spirit, & joy

Create in me a clean heart, O God,
and renew a steadfast spirit within me.
Do not cast me away from Your presence,
and do not take Your Holy Spirit from me.
Restore to me the joy of Your salvation,
and uphold me by Your generous Spirit.

Psalm 51:10-12

Create in me a clean heart, O God, and renew a steadfast spirit within me. Do not cast me away from Your presence, and do not take Your Holy Spirit from me. Restore to me the joy of Your salvation, and uphold me by Your generous Spirit. Psalm 51:10-12

2012   J.V.Wallace

Create In Me

Enter God's rest...
Have faith in who He is
Believe His Word to you
Cease from your own work
Surrender to the will of God

There remains therefore a rest for the people of God.
For he who has entered His rest
has himself also ceased from
his works as God did from His.
Let us therefore be diligent to enter that rest.

Hebrews 4:9-11

Enter His Rest

As you grow in the Lord &
seek the path He has for you
Do not be discouraged or dismayed
Do not forget what He has done
& is doing for you now

Bless the Lord, O my soul; and
all that is within me, bless His holy name!
Bless the Lord, O my soul,
and forget not all His benefits:
Who forgives all your iniquities,
Who heals all your diseases,
Who redeems your life from destruction,
Who crowns you with loving-kindness
and tender mercies,
Who satisfies your mouth with good things,
so that your youth is renewed like the eagle's.

Psalm 103:1-5

Forget Not

Draw close to God through the trials of life
& He will draw close to you
He will set things in order,
complete what is lacking
& make you fully ready
He who calls you is faithful, who also will do it

*But may the God of all grace, who
called us to His eternal glory by Christ Jesus,
after you have suffered a while,
perfect, establish, strengthen, and settle you.*

1 Peter 5:10

God Perfects

Keep your focus on the Risen One
Day & night He is mindful of you
Protecting - Providing - Preserving
The Lord goes before you shining -
making a way where there is no way

I will lift up my eyes to the hills–
from whence comes my help?
My help comes from the LORD,
who made heaven and earth.
He will not allow your foot to be moved;
He who keeps you will not slumber. Behold,
He who keeps Israel shall neither slumber nor sleep.
The LORD is your keeper;
The LORD is your shade at your right hand.
The sun shall not strike you by day, nor the moon by night.
The LORD shall preserve you from all evil;
He shall preserve your soul.
The LORD shall preserve your going out and your coming in
from this time forth, and even forevermore.

Psalm 121

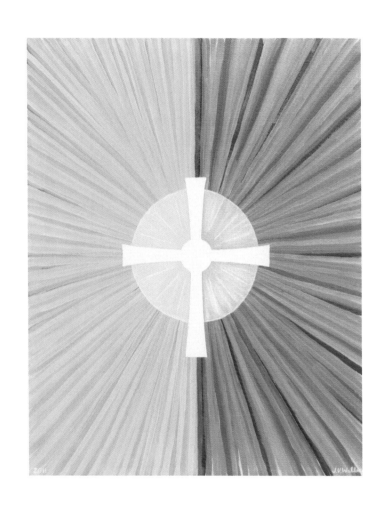

He Shall Preserve

Holdfast to who you are in Christ
& to what He has given you to do
Stay intimately connected with Him
Here you are completely & lovingly cared for
Free to grow while He guides your path

But I am the vine, you are the branches.
He who abides in Me, and I in him, bears much fruit;
for without Me you can do nothing.

John 15:5

He Who Abides

Diligently seek an intimate
relationship with the Lord
He will come to meet with you &
in His perfect timing fulfill all your needs
His faithfulness is as dependable
as the rising of the sun

Let us know,
let us pursue the knowledge of the Lord.
His going forth is established as the morning;
He will come to us like the rain,
like the latter and former rain to the earth.

Hosea 6:3

He Will Come To Us

Seek to abide in the Lord's presence
- Hidden in Him -
Set apart from all that steals your peace
Surround yourself with praise & thankfulness
- Worshiping Him -
Dwelling here brings life & healing
to your body, mind, & soul

You are my hiding place;
You shall preserve me from trouble;
You shall surround me with songs of deliverance.

Psalm 32:7

Hiding Place

Strengthen yourself in the Lord
Don't look at your lack
Refocus
Remember what He has done
Praise the Lord
Hope in Him

Why are you cast down, O my soul?
And why are you disquieted within me?
Hope in God, for I shall yet praise Him
for the help of His countenance.
The Lord will command
His loving-kindness in the daytime,
and in the night His song shall be with me -
a prayer to the God of my life.

Psalm 42:5, 8

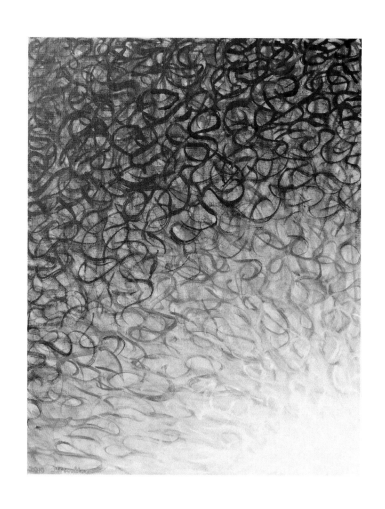

Hope In God

You can take a promise
God has given you &
let it discourage you by focusing
on the delays to destiny
OR
You can let it bring you life
& peace as you trust in
God's goodness & faithfulness
as He brings it to pass

Hope deferred makes the heart sick,
but desire fulfilled is a tree of life.

Proverbs 13:12

Hope Tree

You are no longer bound
by the lies of the enemy
You are free!
Free to be who God created you to be
& in that there is a supernatural joy

These things I have spoken to you,
that My joy may remain in you,
and that your joy may be full.

John 15:11

I Am Free

Your identity is not determined by
who you once were or your circumstances
You are a new creation
Alive & hidden in Christ
See yourself as God sees you &
live as who He created you to be

If then you were raised with Christ,
seek those things which are from above,
where Christ is, sitting at the right hand of God.
Set your mind on things above,
not on things on the earth. For you died,
and your life is hidden with Christ in God.

Colossians 3:1-3

Identity In Christ

Allow Holy Spirit to renew your mind
Releasing life & peace to grow in your heart
Blessing those around you
with His life-giving flow

For to be carnally minded is death, but
to be spiritually minded is life and peace.

Romans 8:6

Life & Peace

You were created to do more than reflect...
You carry God's manifest presence,
power & life!
You are in Him & He shines through you
impacting & transforming everything...
Arise & shine!

You are the light of the world.

Matthew 5:14

For you were once darkness,
but now you are light in the Lord.
Walk as children of light...

Ephesians 5:8

Light

Come out of the desert
Through the cleansing blood
Through the healing waters
Into limitless inheritance
as you follow the Son

Therefore we also, since we are
surrounded by so great a cloud of witnesses,
let us lay aside every weight,
and the sin that so easily ensnares us,
and let us run with endurance
the race that is set before us,
looking unto Jesus
the author and finisher of our faith.

Hebrews 12:1-2a

Looking Unto Jesus

God's heart desire is that you would be free ...
Free from everything
that separates you from Him
Free to receive the love
He has poured out in your heart
Free to become who He created you to be ...
a light shining His glory

Therefore if the Son makes you free,
you shall be free indeed.

John 8:36

Made Free

See yourself as the Lord sees you
Let Him lead you on the path
He has prepared for you
No shame - No comparison
No fear - No doubt
You are free to fly & be
who He has called you to be

Yes, the Lord will give what is good;
and the land will yield its increase.
Righteousness will go before Him,
and shall make His footsteps our pathway.

Psalm 85:12-13

Our Pathway

God is walking with you & working in you
His great love for you
shines brightly in your darkness
Restoring hope to see
His promises for you come to pass!

We also glory in tribulations, knowing that
tribulation produces perseverance;
and perseverance, character;
and character hope.
Now hope does not disappoint,
because the love of God
has been poured out in our hearts
by the Holy Spirit who was given to us.

Romans 5:3-5

Process of Promise

Pursue the Lord...
Hunger & thirst for His presence
& you will be filled
He delights to know you & to be known by you
He desires to help you & to protect you
Pursue the Lord...
Don't settle for less

O, God, You are my God; early will I seek You;
my soul thirsts for You; my flesh longs for You
in a dry and thirsty land where there is no water.
So I have looked for You in the sanctuary,
to see Your power and Your glory.
You have been my help, therefore
in the shadow of Your wings I will rejoice.
My soul follows close behind You;
Your right hand upholds me.

Psalm 63:1-2, 7-8

Pursue The Lord

I am not moved by my feelings
nor circumstances
I am confident & secure for I know
Whose I am & who I am in Him
I am not striving to be accepted
nor to figure things out
I am submitted & committed to what
God has given me to do
while I expectantly wait for Him
to bring His good plan to pass

Lord, my heart is not haughty, nor my eyes lofty.
Neither do I concern myself with great matters,
nor with things too profound for me.
Surely I have calmed and quieted my soul,
like a weaned child with his mother;
like a weaned child is my soul within me.
O Israel, hope in the Lord from
this time forth and forever. - Psalm 131

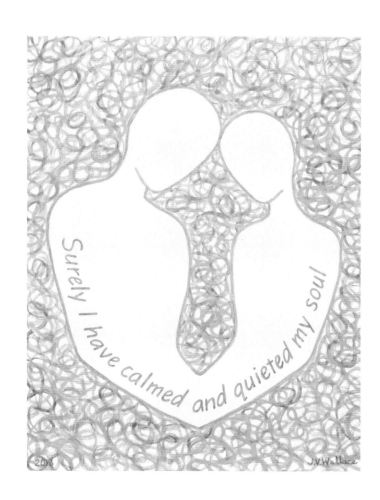

Surely I have calmed and quieted my soul

Quieted My Soul

Let God's joy and peace fill you
Keeping your hope steadfast in Him
Bringing life, healing, restoration

Restore us, O God;
cause Your face to shine,
and we shall be saved!

Psalm 80:3

May the God of hope fill you with
all joy and peace as you trust in Him,
so that you may overflow with hope
by the power of the Holy Spirit.

Romans 15:13

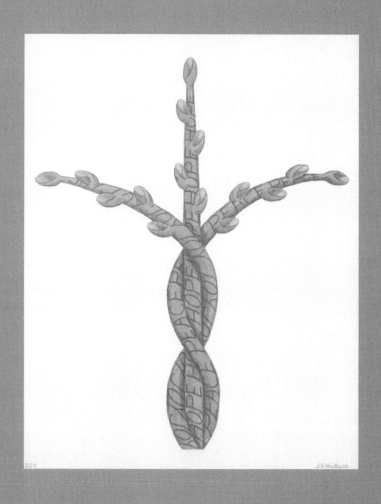

Restore Us

The Lord has placed desires in your heart
Sow these seeds
Let Him resurrect them
Creating new life
He has prepared the soil &
will send the rain, wind & sun
The Lord has a good plan for you
& will be faithful to complete it

*Most assuredly I say to you, unless a grain of wheat
falls into the ground and dies, it remains alone;
but if it dies, it produces much grain.*

John 12:24

Resurrection & Life

Withdraw from the busyness of life
Retreat into the tranquil presence of the Lord
Be still
Let go
Trust Him
Be at peace
He will revive your soul &
draw you deeper into wholeness in Him

In returning and rest you shall be saved;
In quietness and confidence shall be your strength.

Isaiah 30:15

Returning & Rest

Be a good steward of what
God has entrusted to you
Your heart is a safe place to
preserve & nurture His word
He has given you until it is birthed
This requires great faith & trust

Trust in the Lord, and do good;
dwell in the land, and feed on His faithfulness.
Delight yourself also in the Lord, and
He shall give you the desires of your heart.
Commit your way to the Lord,
trust also in Him, and He shall bring it to pass.

Psalm 37:3-5

Seeds of Inheritance

The Lord is testing what you trust in
& your foundation
He desires right-relationship with you
because you are His -
chosen, holy, & beloved

In the Lord I put my trust;
How can you say to my soul,
"Flee as a bird to your mountain?"
If the foundations are destroyed,
what can the righteous do?
The Lord tests the righteous.
For the Lord is righteous,
He loves righteousness;
His countenance beholds the upright.

Psalm 11: 1, 3, 5, 7

The Lord Tests

It's a new season for the Lord's people -
turning hearts back to the Kingdom
A time of healing, adjustments,
building character, maturing
So rest encouraged & strengthened in Him
The seed is already in the ground

The kingdom of God is as if a man
should scatter seed on the ground,
and should sleep by night and rise by day,
and the seed should sprout and grow,
he himself does not know how.

Mark 4:26-27

The Seed Should Sprout

Rely on God's character & ability to do
what He has given you to do today
Enjoy where you are at
Be thankful - Pursue knowing God
Give your cares completely to Him
Let joy & peace fill you each day
knowing He is with you
bringing His good plan to pass

Trust in the Lord, and do good;
dwell in the land, and feed on His faithfulness.
Delight yourself also in the Lord, and
He shall give you the desires of your heart.
Commit your way to the Lord,
trust also in Him, and He shall bring it to pass.
He shall bring forth your righteousness as
the light, and your justice as the noonday.
Rest in the Lord, and wait patiently for Him.

Psalm 37:3-7a

Trust In The Lord

wallace designs

art revealing the kingdom

the art & ministry of
Jennifer V. Wallace
www.wallacedesigns.com

"The Spirit of the LORD is upon Me,
Because He has anointed Me to
preach the gospel to the poor;
He has sent Me to heal the brokenhearted,
To proclaim liberty to the captives
and recovery of sight to the blind,
To set at liberty those who are oppressed;
To proclaim the acceptable year of the LORD."
Luke 4:18-19